How to Understand Your Bible

Alan Stibbs

Revised By David & Clare Wenham

Harold Shaw Publishers
Wheaton, Illinois

Copyright © 1950, Inter-Varsity Press, England
as UNDERSTANDING GOD'S WORD
Revised edition © 1976
ISBN 0-85110-386-3

Published in North America as
HOW TO UNDERSTAND YOUR BIBLE
by special arrangement with
Inter-Varsity Press, England

First printing, 1977

ISBN 0-87788-365-3
Library of Congress Catalog Card Number 77-72351

Printed in the United States of America

Preface

Alan Stibbs, once a missionary in China and later for
many years Vice-Principal of Oak Hill Theological
College, London, was well known and much loved as a
Bible expositor. His book *Understanding God's Word*
in its first edition (1950) has proved a valuable handbook for thousands of Bible students. It might seem
unnecessary to undertake a revision of such a book, and
certainly it was no easy task. But inevitably the book
has become dated to some extent, and it was felt that
it could be made more useful to today's Bible students
if it were thoroughly revised and updated.

The result is a book that in some respects is quite
different from its first edition, although it is closely
modelled on the original, adopting its general pattern
and incorporating most of its contents. We have not
attempted to imitate the author's style, and yet most of
the ideas and many of the words are his. There has been
much reshaping, rearranging and at times expansion of
material, particularly in the middle chapters; new
examples and some other new material have been
inserted where it was thought necessary. Nevertheless
we have not felt free to depart far from the original by
introducing a large amount of new material.

We hope that this new edition will not offend those who loved the old, but that the changes will give the book the new lease of life that it deserves, and make it more widely useful to a new generation of Bible students.

Our thanks are due to Mrs Olive Stibbs who kindly agreed to the updating of her husband's book and read through the manuscript.

Finally, we echo Alan Stibbs's prayer for the use of *Understanding God's Word*, quoted from his preface to the first edition: 'May God Himself increase proper understanding and profitable use of His Word by all ways and by all means; and may the reading of this book lead some to a new and better use of such ways and means.'

David and Clare Wenham

Yeotmal, Maharashtra, India

Using the Bible properly

1

The Bible is one of the greatest treasures that the Christian possesses. Few things are more important for the life of the church and of the individual Christian than using it properly.

The apostle Paul explained the value of the Bible for the Christian when he wrote to Timothy: 'All scripture is inspired by God and profitable for teaching, for reproof, for correction, and for training in righteousness, that the man of God may be complete, equipped for every good work' (2 Tim. 3:16, 17). In other words, the Bible is a textbook given by God, through which we learn first what to believe and second how to live. In it we learn the truth about God, about what he has done to save us through the life, death and resurrection of Jesus Christ; in it we have a pattern for living, an authoritative rule of faith and a final court of appeal in questions of right and wrong.

We have, then, a great responsibility to use the Bible properly. Because we believe that it is inspired by God we must approach it reverently and humbly; we must seek to understand it accurately; we must obey it ourselves and pass its truths on to others by word and action. If we are really seeking to base our lives on God's Word and to explain its teaching to others, therefore, we must first take care that our understanding of the Bible message is a true one.

We must not approach the Bible carelessly and casually, presuming to know what its message is without first taking great pains to discover exactly what it teaches. Because we all have our prejudices and misconceptions, it is all too easy to see in Scripture only what we want to see, and to miss the revelation of God's fuller truth which is his purpose for us, but which depends on our using his Word rightly. What is even worse, it is all too easy to use Scripture as a sort of peg on which to hang our own ideas, instead of getting out of it what it actually does teach, which may contradict our own ideas. Such handling of God's Word is a presumptuous imposition on Scripture of personal prejudice instead of a proper humble exposition of God-given revelation.

We will not reach the goal of an accurate understanding of the Bible without effort; the search for understanding demands prayerfulness, hard work and persistence. That does not mean that it is only intellectuals who can understand; God rewards all who honestly and faithfully seek him and will speak to them through his Word. What is required of everyone, however, is that we do not rest satisfied with the limited knowledge that we have.

Although the gift of understanding the Bible is entirely from God, we still have to work in order to grow in understanding. It is the same with all God's gifts: he gives, but we have to be active if we are to enjoy the benefits of his giving. Similarly, the farmer must work in the fields sowing, weeding and harvesting. If he fails to do what is necessary at each stage, the harvest may be spoiled. So, if our lives are to yield their full harvest to

God's glory, we must work; and that work involves working to understand the Word of God.

There is, therefore, much need for us all to be 'disciples' before we become 'apostles'. We need to spend much time as students in God's school if we are to do God's will in the world and to stand before men as true ministers of the gospel. In other words, that true understanding of the Bible, which is absolutely essential to its right use, cannot be gained just by offering a prayer before we read. We must be prepared to take time and trouble, using our God-given powers of intelligence and judgment as we read and study it.

The purpose of this book is to give some basic guidance and practical suggestions to those who are prepared to join the school of biblical understanding. Let us remember what the apostle Paul said to Timothy: 'Do your best to present yourself to God as one approved, a workman who has no need to be ashamed, rightly handling the word of truth' (2 Tim. 2:15).

Getting at the true text

2

When people attempt to define the Bible's inspiration they sometimes include the statement that the words were inspired 'as originally given'. This is just another way of recognizing that we do not have the original manuscripts of the biblical books, but only copies and translations of the original texts. Inevitably in the process of copying out the texts again and again, often by hand, errors of various kinds have crept into many manuscripts; and translations, however accurate, often fail to capture the full flavour of the original.

Here, however, we can at once recognize with gratitude God's amazing providence in connection with his written Word. The text of the Bible is far better preserved than that of most other ancient writings.[1] Also the content of the original lends itself to translation. For the Bible is not a book full of abstract or philosophical language that is difficult to understand or express in different languages and cultural situations; it is a book of real-life examples and concrete history. And because its vivid idioms and illustrations are taken from everyday life they can still be appreciated hundreds

[1] For fuller details see F. F. Bruce, *The New Testament Documents*[5] (IVP, 1960), chapter 2.

of years after they were written, and appeal to people from widely differing backgrounds.

The language

Today most of us rely to a greater or lesser extent on translations, since biblical Hebrew and Greek are no longer in current use. These translations are numerous and varied: some attempt a fairly literal translation, following the original Hebrew and Greek closely (*e.g.*, Revised Version, Revised Standard Version); others are more free and try to use English that will be more easily understood by modern readers (*e.g.*, J. B. Phillips, New English Bible, Today's English Version). There is value in both kinds of translation, and one of the best ways of increasing our understanding of the original is to compare one version with another. (This applies to paraphrases and commentaries as well.)

Most of the translations available are the result of a great deal of research and scholarship. If it were not for this painstaking study by many scholars over many centuries we would not be able to read the Bible in our own language at all. But all translations, even the best, have their limitations. For example, it is often quite impossible for a translator to find words which adequately express some fine shade of meaning in the original. He has to be content with conveying the general sense, or even sometimes with a mere suggestion of the meaning. In different contexts the same word in the original may have to be translated by different words in English. Alternatively, different words in the original may be translated by the same word in English. It follows that suggestions in the original either of similarity or of difference may be lost or even contradicted in the process of translation. This is not the translator's fault. He can only do his best with the words at his disposal.

This means that if we are to be able to explain to others exactly what the Bible teaches we must ourselves get beyond the limitations of translations and paraphrases to a more exact appreciation of the meaning of the original. To do this we must make good use of all the aids now available.

Best of all is to know Hebrew and Greek ourselves, and this is not as impossible as it may sound![2] As a good second best, however, it is possible to go a long way towards an accurate understanding of the original by using some of the many study aids that are available. For example, an analytical concordance[3] provides a transliteration of the Hebrew and Greek words and so enables us to see when the same or different words are used in the original, and gives us a clue as to the particular shade of meaning of a certain word. Good commentaries are invaluable for explaining the significance of different words and phrases, and will often help us to understand the differences between the different translations.

The text

Commentaries will also give us information about the findings of the textual critics. Textual criticism is the art of trying to establish the original text of the biblical books, and as such is constructive rather than des-

[2] Those who have taken the trouble to learn one or both of these languages have found the effort involved abundantly worth while when it comes to serious Bible study. In some towns evening classes are available, and a number of Bible colleges offer correspondence courses.

[3] *E.g.*, R. Young, *Analytical Concordance to the Holy Bible* (Lutterworth Press, 1879) and J. Strong, *The Exhaustive Concordance of the Bible* (Hodder and Stoughton, 1894).

tructive. Those who undertake this work must be specialists who not only know the original languages, but who have become skilled in reading and comparing ancient manuscripts. Their work involves them in identifying the various alternative readings, and also in detecting the obvious copying errors and possible later emendations, *i.e.*, places where a scribe seems to have tried to 'improve' the text by simplifying a difficulty or by trying to correct a previous scribe's mistake. Textual critics will often have to choose between two or more alternative readings, all of which may be found in ancient manuscripts; and sometimes, when there is a particular difficulty in the text which we have, they may suggest a possible emendation or more likely reading.

Manuscripts tend to fall into groups. Those which share many of the same features and variant readings in their text presumably had a common origin; they bear witness together to one comparatively early form of the text. After manuscripts have been classified and grouped in this way, the different variations of reading which each group represents still have to be compared. In choosing between them the generally accepted rule is to prefer the more difficult reading, simply because it is more likely that a scribe altered a passage to make it less difficult than that one altered it to make it more so.

The choice between different readings may very occasionally become more than a matter of textual criticism alone. It may need the judgment of the New Testament historian and theologian. Both could have grounds other than those of the immediate manuscript evidence for expressing a preference for a particular reading or translation.

These discrepancies between manuscripts have served a most beneficial purpose. They have awakened and stimulated intellectual inquiry and investigation which in turn have brought results of great value. We are now more sure of the text of the original Scriptures than were previous generations. We know how amazingly well the Bible text has been preserved. As Christians we have every right to say that our documentary evidence is so outstandingly good that it is in a class by itself. The margin of possible error is virtually negligible. And a remarkable fact about the preservation of the text is that no doctrine is called in question by textual uncertainties.

Christians who love and honour the Bible as the inspired Word of God have sometimes been suspicious of criticism of all sorts, supposing it to be something destructive and rationalistic. But textual criticism is an example of thoroughly constructive biblical criticism which should be welcomed, not feared.[4] Christians who

[4] Many people suppose that biblical criticism means criticizing the Bible in the sense of trying to find fault with it, and they are naturally suspicious of it for that reason. But biblical criticism may be more accurately defined as the scholarly study of the history and development of the biblical writings. Thus, as we have seen, *textual criticism* is the study of the history and development of the biblical books after they were written down. *Source criticism* and *form criticism* ask about the history of the contents of the Bible before they were written down by the biblical authors. From what sources, *e.g.*, did Luke get the stories which he put in the book of Acts – from personal interviews with eyewitnesses, from traditions passed down in the church, from earlier written records, or from where? *Redaction criticism* is the study of the way in which the biblical authors have edited (or 'redacted') their sources. The redaction critic seeks to understand why a particular writer included in his book one story and not another, why he arranged his material in a particular way, and so on.

Such study of the different ways that God worked in and through human beings to give us the Bible is quite compatible with a belief in its divine inspiration, and our understanding of the Bible can be greatly enriched through the critics' work. But it should be added that many critics have come to the Bible with un-Christian presuppositions, *e.g.*, with a rationalistic prejudice against miracles and without a belief in Scripture as God's infallible Word; their findings have often been negative as a result. The Christian student needs to

accept the Bible as God's Word written ought to be committed to and involved in such research work. They of all people should be willing to sweat and toil in their efforts to establish both what Scripture says and what it means. Many are now involved in such work, but there is a continuing need for biblical scholars whose concern is to bring the Word of God to his church and to his world.

---

discriminate between the good and the bad so as not to reject the one or to swallow the other!

Understanding a passage
in its context

3

When we come to study a passage in the Bible, we must
make sure that we thoroughly understand the writer's
original meaning before we attempt to apply his teaching more widely. This will involve, first, reading the
passage through as a whole and studying its context,
which is the subject of this chapter, and, second, looking
at it in closer detail. This is discussed in the next chapter.

*1. Get to know the background to the Old and New
Testaments – the customs, ways of life, geographical
setting, etc.* Without this you could easily miss the force
of allusions and expressions which would have been
obvious to the original readers of the passage you are
studying. This is, of course, a long-term aim; no-one
can be expected to grasp the whole background to a
passage in one sitting! It is also, as the following
examples will suggest, an almost inexhaustible field of
study. Nevertheless, there is a wide variety of books at
different levels which will help you gradually to build
up a picture of life in biblical times.[1]

[1] For a popular, illustrated handbook in full colour which is most
useful, see *The Lion Handbook to the Bible* (Lion Publishing, 1973).
Other books include R. K. Harrison, *Old Testament Times* (IVP,
1971); Merrill C. Tenney, *New Testament Times* (IVP, 1961) and

Examples. The more we can find out about the climate and scenery of the Bible lands, about the different cities and towns and their relationship to each other, the more we shall be able to picture in our minds the setting of the Bible. We shall (for instance) be able to follow the travels of Abraham, Paul and Jesus himself; we shall be able to appreciate the complaints of the Israelites as they wandered in the bleak, barren wilderness (see, *e.g.*, Ex. 16:1–3; 17:1–4); we shall be able to grasp the full force of the many examples of imagery connected with thirst, water in the desert, *etc.*, which those who live in temperate climates with adequate rainfall might miss (see, *e.g.*, Ps. 63:1; Is. 41:17, 18; 44:3, 4).[2]

If we understand something of the religions of the ancient Near East, with their sexual licence, cult prostitution and child-sacrifice, it will help us to see why the Old Testament is so bitterly opposed to them (see, *e.g.*, Dt. 7:1–5; Ezr. 9:1, 2, 10–15).[3] A command such as 'You shall not boil a kid in its mother's milk' (Ex. 23:19), which seems to us to be rather a strange thing to prohibit, makes some sense when we realize that this was a practice associated with pagan fertility rites. Some of the poetic references to the monsters 'Rahab' and 'Leviathan' (*e.g.*, Is. 51:9; Ps. 74:14) may be explicable

New Testament Survey (IVP, 1965); J. D. Douglas (ed.), *The New Bible Dictionary* (IVP, 1962), a valuable reference book for the Bible student.

[2] Looking at pictures of the places mentioned in the Bible (if you cannot actually visit them for yourself) will help a great deal here. For excellent colour photographs see *The Lion Handbook of the Bible*, mentioned above, and also *Photo-Guide to the Old Testament* (Lion Publishing, 1973) and *Photo-Guide to the New Testament* (Lion Publishing, 1972). See also the various Bible atlases available, *e.g.*, L. H. Grolenberg, *Atlas of the Bible* (Nelson, 1956), which contains both maps and photographs.

[3] See further J. W. Wenham, *The Goodness of God* (IVP, 1974), chapter 8, 'The Abominations of the Heathen'.

from the myths of ancient Babylon. Some of the language of the myths, but not their substance, is found from time to time in the Old Testament.[4]

Similarly, the New Testament is full of allusions and references to Jewish beliefs and practices; we should therefore try to learn as much as we can about first- and second-century Judaism. A knowledge of Graeco-Roman religion, too, will throw light on, for example, some of Paul's references (*e.g.*, 1 Cor. 8:1, 10, *etc.*). Paul's language in some of his Letters, *e.g.*, his frequent use of such words as 'knowledge' (*gnōsis*), 'wisdom' (*sophia*) and 'mystery' (*mystērion*), may have been taken over from the Gnostic beliefs of some of his opponents and used against them (see, *e.g.*, Col. 2:2–4, 8).[5]

A statement such as 'Boaz went to the gate and sat down' (Ru. 4:1; *cf.* Pr. 24:7, 'in the gate he does not open his mouth'; and 2 Sa. 15:2 ff.) becomes clear when we understand that the city gate was the main place of assembly where legal and other business was transacted. In New Testament times, however, the market place was the main public gathering-place where preliminary trial hearings and public and informal discussions were held. Thus Paul, while he was in Athens, argued and discussed 'in the market place every day with those who chanced to be there' (Acts 17:17).

2. *Aim to discover the circumstances of writing and the situations being addressed.* When studying a particular passage, we must try to establish who the writer was, and who were the people for whom he was writing. We need to try to step into the writer's shoes, to understand his situation and his outlook, and to appreciate his

---

[4] See, *e.g.*, 'Rahab', *The New Bible Dictionary*, p. 1074b.
[5] See, *e.g.*, 'Gnosticism', *The New Bible Dictionary*, pp. 473 f.; 'Colossians', section VI, *ibid.*, p. 243b.

attitude to prevailing circumstances. Reading the Old Testament historical books will help us to understand better the situation addressed by the various prophets. A good grasp of the course of events recorded in Acts is essential as the background to some of Paul's Letters. Since these are dealing with specific conditions, problems and errors in particular churches at that time, we cannot hope fully to understand or appreciate them unless we first find out all we can about their background. Here commentaries are a tremendous help, particularly the introductory sections dealing with the date and circumstances of writing.

3. Have regard to the author's purpose in writing the book. The author's aims may be expressly mentioned, as in Luke 1:1-4 or John 20:31. But often it can be appreciated only by careful study. It is important to get some idea not only of the author's over-all purpose in a book but also his intentions in particular sections of his work. To read texts in isolation and out of context is a sure way to misunderstanding.

Examples. In the book of Job it would be easy to take some of the words of Job's friends out of context and to think that they were the inspired message of the book. But the author intends us to regard them as worldly, and not divine, wisdom, as we discover when we read Job 42:7-9.

Psalms 120–134, the 'Songs of Degrees' or 'Ascents', were probably written to be used by the pilgrims on their way up to Jerusalem for the great festivals. The significance of some of the verses (see especially Ps. 122) can be appreciated only when this is recognized.

Romans 3:28 and James 2:24 are sometimes quoted as contradictory. A study of the two Letters, however, shows that the larger purpose of the writer was different in each case. While Paul was attacking works which claim to take the place of faith as the ground of salvation, James is protesting against that kind of empty profession of faith, or 'barren orthodoxy', which does not express response to God in active obedience and therefore is not the faith which saves. *Cf.* Romans 4:1–5 and James 2:21–23.

4. Have regard to the kind of literature you are reading, and remember that literary customs in Old and New Testament times were not always the same as our own. In order fully to grasp the writer's aim, you must find out whether he is writing history, prophecy, poetry, apocalyptic, wisdom literature, a letter, and so on. Try also to understand something of the general characteristics of these and of the methods of writing them. The following brief notes may help.

a. History. History is central to the Christian faith, because God has been revealed through historical people and historical events. Much of the Bible is devoted to describing this revelation of God; these parts should be taken seriously as the history of God's dealings with his people and not treated simply as books full of interesting moral tales. But, although the biblical historians were concerned to tell us what happened in the past, they were not primarily concerned, as modern historians might be, with economic and political issues, nor do they always intend to give precise information on chronology or numbers. Much of Old Testament historical writing was in fact called 'prophecy' by the Jews, as the author's intention was not to record history for its own sake, but to instruct and build up their readers in the faith by teaching people about God's dealings in the past, and by interpreting history. We should not, therefore, demand from biblical historians information which it is not their intention to tell us.

Examples. Reading the Bible's account of the reign of Omri in 1 Kings 16:16–28, one might get the impression, judging it by modern standards, that Omri was an insignificant king. He was, in fact, a rich, powerful and influential one, but he 'did more evil than all who were before him' and is therefore not given a prominent place in the chronicle of God's dealings with Israel.

Similarly, the Gospels should not be regarded as biography in the modern sense: the evangelists do not give us details of Jesus' childhood, his appearance, *etc*. They are bringing out the theological significance, the 'good news' about Jesus, and so they concentrate on what they see as the most important events and sayings of his ministry. This is why, for example, they put particular stress on his death.

The incorporation of whole sections verbatim from other writers without specific acknowledgment was not regarded as improper plagiarism as it would be today. Similarly, two different accounts of the same event may be put alongside each other without any attempt to reconcile or combine them. As with the parallelism of Hebrew poetry, the two expressions are not reduced to a single composite picture by the author, but are left side by side so that the reader can get more from the two together than from one alone.

Examples. Jeremiah 52 quotes 2 Kings 24:18—25:30. Most scholars believe that Matthew and Luke have based their Gospels on Mark's.

In Judges 4 and 5 we have two descriptions of Israel's victory over Sisera and the Canaanites, the first a prose

23

account by the author of Judges, the second a poetic song of Deborah and Barak. (*Cf.* also Gn. 1:1 ff. and 2:4 ff. where we find two different but complementary accounts of creation side by side.)

b. Prophecy. We tend today to think of prophets as men who foretold the future. But we shall miss the point of Old Testament prophecy if we just look for future predictions, remarkable and important though these may be. The prophets were not only men with God-given foresight; just as important, they were men with hindsight and insight into God's past and present activity. They were 'forth-tellers' who spoke about the situation of their day – about the sins of the people and about the will of God – and not just 'foretellers' of the future. The parallels between the situations addressed by the prophets and our situation today are often striking, and we desperately need to listen to what the prophets had and have to say.

The relevance of the prophetic forth-telling to those who heard it first and to us today is clear enough; but what of the foretelling? Why were the prophets allowed to see and to proclaim God's future purposes and plan? It was not so that they might satisfy people's curiosity; rather they were commanded to speak of God's future because of the immediate relevance of that future to the present. It was the revelation that God was going to act in future judgment that gave urgent force to the prophets' call to the people to repent. It was the revelation that God would one day redeem his people that was the basis of the prophets' message of hope to the faithful.

So the predictions of the prophets were intensely relevant to those who heard them; they enabled them, if they were willing, to prepare for what was coming.

For us who live on the other side of the fulfilment of many of the Old Testament prophecies, they may not all be a guide to future events, but they are still of value in reminding us of the nature of our God: he is the Lord of the future and the Lord of history, and he reveals himself and his will to his people.[6]

c. *Poetry*. Some of the Old Testament books are mainly, if not entirely, poetic; see, for example, Job, Psalms, Proverbs, Song of Solomon and many of the prophets. When we read the Bible's poetry, we must try to be sensitive to the poetic language and not attempt to interpret its details literalistically.

Hebrew poetry is characterized by its figurative language,[7] by its rhythm of stresses on certain syllables (which is not always distinguishable in translation), and particularly by its 'parallelism', in which two (or more) lines of verse are grouped together and the first is echoed, complemented, developed or contrasted by those that follow. When we come across this, we must remember that it is a poetic device, and should not

---

[6] In the Bible's view predictive prophecy also has value as evidence in two ways. If events which a prophet could not normally have predicted accurately turn out the way he predicted, this can be seen as telling us (1) something about the prophet – that he was a true and inspired man of God (*cf.* Dt. 18:21, 22; Is. 41:21–23), and (2) something about the events – that they should be understood in the light of the prophet's predictions. The second type of evidential argument is especially prominent in the New Testament: Jesus' fulfilment of Old Testament predictions and types (see further below on typology, chapter 5, section 5b) is seen as important evidence that he is the Lord and Christ looked forward to in the Old Testament (see, *e.g.*, Mt. 21:4 f.; Acts 13:32–41). Both sorts of argument, though they are frequently neglected and though they need to be used with care, are still of value today.

For further discussion of the interpretation of prophecy, see chapter 5, section 5a, below.

[7] On figurative language, see below, chapter 4, section 2b.

attempt to read too much into, for example, the subtle difference between two synonyms.[8]

Examples. In the first example there are two synonymous statements in the second the parallelism works up to a climax; in the third there is a direct contrast.

> Thou didst forgive the iniquity of thy people;
>> thou didst pardon all their sin.
> Thou didst withdraw all thy wrath;
>> thou didst turn from thy hot anger (Ps. 85:2, 3).

> The floods have lifted up, O Lord,
>> the floods have lifted up their voice,
>> the floods lift up their roaring (Ps. 93:3).

> The wicked borrows, and cannot pay back,
>> but the righteous is generous and gives (Ps. 37: 21).

d. Apocalyptic. The books of Daniel and Revelation are outstanding examples within the Bible of a type of Jewish literature generally called 'apocalyptic'. The word 'apocalypse' means 'revelation', and apocalyptic characteristically contains accounts of supernatural revelations or visions, usually about things to come, given by God to the writer often through an angel. To the modern reader the most remarkable thing about apocalyptic is, perhaps, its vivid and extraordinary symbolism. It 'abounds in beasts and seals, in rivers and mountains and stars, in personages celestial and infernal',[9] and also in the use of numbers (*e.g.*, number

---

[8] See Derek Kidner's brief section 'Hebrew Poetry', in *Psalms 1–72* (Tyndale Commentary; IVP, 1973), pp. 1 ff. For another short introduction, see F. F. Bruce, 'The Poetry of the Old Testament', in *The New Bible Commentary Revised* (IVP, 1970), pp. 44 ff.

[9] Leon Morris, *Apocalyptic* (IVP, 1974), p. 37. This book is useful as an introduction to the whole subject.

seven in Revelation). Such pictorial language enables the writer to portray whole movements of history and supernatural realities that could not otherwise easily be explained. The characteristic hope of the apocalyptists is for God's final and certain victory over all evil and rebellion in his creation.

For the interpretation of apocalyptic two things are essential. First, the reader must recognize that apocalyptic is a distinctive type of literature and not interpret it as though it were to be taken literally. Second, he must seek to learn as much as possible about the significance of the symbolism used (*e.g.*, a 'beast' is frequently used in apocalyptic to stand for a nation). This can be achieved partly through a study of biblical apocalyptic, and partly by consulting commentaries and works of reference which will bring to bear the evidence from extra-biblical sources.

It may be well to add a note of caution here. There are two dangers for the Christian faced with the phenomenon of apocalyptic. On the one hand he may find it strange and therefore ignore it; but by doing this he is neglecting a significant part of God's revealed truth. On the other hand he may get excessively fascinated by it, giving it a larger place in his thinking than can be justified from Scripture itself. Our Lord used apocalyptic himself (*e.g.*, Mk. 13), but he also warned against those who speculate foolishly about the end (*e.g.*, Mt. 24:26 ff.; Mk. 13:4 ff.) and explained that it is not for man to know about the dates and times which the Father has set within his own control (Acts 1:7).

d. Wisdom literature.[1] The books of Job, Proverbs and

---

[1] For a brief introduction, see F. F. Bruce, 'The Wisdom Literature of the Old Testament', in *The New Bible Commentary Revised*, pp. 48 ff.

Ecclesiastes fall into the distinctive category of wisdom literature, a form of writing found in other Near Eastern literature as well as in the Bible. Wisdom contains careful observation and reflective thinking about life, whether about life as a whole (as in Ecclesiastes), about a particular problem in life (*e.g.*, the problem of suffering, as in Job), or about practical questions of everyday life (as in many of the Proverbs). It often has a distinctive literary form: Job is a series of poetic discourses which put different and opposing points of view; Proverbs contains some thematic discourses (*e.g.*, on the good wife, 31:10–31) but also many short, pithy proverbs (*e.g.*, chapter 10).

Once again it is important to recognize the type of literature when it is found. It would be a mistake, for example, to treat Ecclesiastes as though it were a straight philosophical statement about life, instead of as an account of a man's struggle with the question of meaning in life. Similarly, it would be a mistake to take Proverbs as though it were a book of instructions to the Christian of the same sort as Paul's instructions to Christian churches. Often a proverb is more an observation about life than a command to be obeyed, and it needs to be interpreted accordingly. So far as Job is concerned, it is obviously important to recognize that opposing points of view are being put forward by different speakers; the interpreter will miss the point of the book if he fails to differentiate between the views being criticized as inadequate and those being recommended.

e. Letters. There were a number of formal rules for letter-writing in biblical times, just as there are to a lesser extent today. Paul follows the normal practice of his day in the way in which he begins and ends his

Letters, and also in his dictation of them to a scribe, adding only a personal postscript or salutation in his own handwriting (see Rom. 16:22; Col. 4:18; 2 Thes. 3:1 f.).

In some parts of his Letters, as one might expect, Paul answers points from a letter that has been sent to him (see, *e.g.*, 1 Cor. 7:1 ff.). In 1 Corinthians he appears to be going through a letter from the church in Corinth, answering it point by point (see 1 Cor. 7:1; 8:1; 12:1; 16:1) and sometimes quoting from it (see 1 Cor. 8:1, 4). If we try to appreciate the circumstances and methods of writing, we will not make the mistake of, for example, taking Paul's Letters as exhaustive discourses on a certain subject, but rather as practical advice given to a specific situation.

Understanding a passage in detail

4

After considering a passage in its wider context, we are in a position to look at smaller sections of it in greater detail. The following are some general rules.

1. Notice the form and structure of the passage – the connections of thought, the main thrust of the argument, etc. This will be easier if the passage has first been considered in its over-all context, as suggested in the previous chapter. Do not be misled by chapter and verse divisions, which were added long after the original was written to make quotation of specific verses easier.

Examples. A comparison of 1 Corinthians 1:12 and 3:21, 22 shows that in the latter verses Paul still has the same subject in mind. His statement that 'All things are yours, whether Paul or Apollos or Cephas or the world of life or death or the present or the future', cannot be understood without appreciating that the whole of 1 Corinthians 1:10—4:21 is about ministers, their message and their ministry. This is why the Christians are wrong to say 'I belong to Paul' or 'I belong to Apollos', for Paul's argument, summed up in 3:22, is that ministers belong to the Christians whom they are serving and not Christians to their ministers.

Similarly, if a sentence includes a 'therefore', we should try to understand it in the light of what has gone before, even if it is at the beginning of a chapter (see, *e.g.*, Rom. 5:1; 8:1; Heb. 4:1; 6:1). Do not let chapter divisions obscure the continuation of an argument. This is particularly important in Paul's Letters, where his argument is often complex and where, as we saw in the example above, he may return to his main subject after a number of intermediate arguments; *cf.* also 1 Corinthians 10:14, which returns, after some related discussion, to the subject of food offered to idols, first raised in 8:1 ff.

2. Recognize the type of literature and interpret it accordingly. We have already outlined the main categories of literature into which a book may fall.[1] Within that book, however, there may be different types of writing. In a historical book, for example, you may find genealogies and snatches of poetry, as well as all sorts of figurative language. These types of literature need to be recognized and appreciated for what they are, or you may end up, for example, interpreting a parable as history, and thus missing the point completely.

a. Genealogies are not intended to be complete; they are specially selected to establish someone's descent from a particular ancestor.
Example. Jesus' descent from Abraham and from David is traced in three sets of 'fourteen generations' in Matthew 1:1 ff. It is thought that fourteen may have been chosen because the numerical value of the Hebrew word 'David' is fourteen and this would further stress Jesus' royalty.

[1] See chapter 3, section 4.

b. Figurative language. The most obvious type of writing which requires special care in interpretation is figurative language, in which the Bible abounds. God is seen as a rock, a fortress, a shield, a shepherd. Israel is described as a vineyard, the good man as a tree flourishing at the water's edge, the devil as a roaring lion on the prowl for its prey. Jesus describes himself as the bread of life, as living water, as the door of the sheepfold, and he puts much of his teaching into parables, stories drawn from everyday experience.

This kind of language is common in all cultures. We use it, often unconsciously, as we try to describe a new experience or an unusual event in terms of what we have already experienced, or of things the hearer knows. In literature, and particularly in poetry, figurative language has for centuries played a vital part in enriching the language, and making descriptions all the more vivid.

The Bible, then, is making use of a method of communication which is readily understandable to all. Its teaching, illustrated by word pictures drawn from the countryside and from home life, has direct relevance to ordinary human interests and makes an impression on the mind which can easily be recalled. This is no doubt one of the reasons why Jesus made such frequent use of parables to put his message across. Figurative language is all the more appropriate in the Bible, since it is dealing with truths which were hitherto unknown, with things that cannot fully be expressed in factual language, and which cannot properly be understood by finite minds, subjects such as the character of God and the nature of the heavenly realm.

To understand figurative language we need to study the way it is used in Scripture, so that we come to recognize particular metaphors (such as the vine standing for Israel, which is found throughout the Bible; see, *e.g.*, Is. 5:1 ff.; Ho. 10:1 ff.; *cf.* Jn. 15:1–11). We need also to study the background to the Old and New Testaments, so that we can appreciate the figurative expressions used. Especially in the industrialized western world with its tendency to use matter-of-fact language, we may fail to appreciate the more 'flowery' language or the figures drawn from eastern customs and surroundings.

Example. The Bible idea of a dog is completely different from ours. In contrast to the well-trained, pampered house dogs of the West today, in the East dogs were – and still are in some places – simply a menace to be driven out of the city during the day, only to steal back under cover of darkness, when they could be heard howling or growling over their food. Thus Revelation 22:15 says of the heavenly city: 'Outside are the dogs and sorcerers and fornicators and murderers.' In Psalm 59:6 David says of his enemies: 'Each evening they come back, howling like dogs and prowling about the city.' In contrast, when Jesus spoke to the Syrophoenician woman of 'throwing food to the dogs' (see Mk. 7:24–30), the word used is the diminutive, 'little dogs' or 'puppies'. Whereas fully grown dogs would not be allowed in the house to be stroked and fed, puppies were. So the woman was encouraged to answer, 'Even the puppies under the table eat the children's crumbs.'

Various different types of figurative language may be distinguished.

(*i*.) *Simple figures and word pictures*. These occur on almost every page of the Bible, especially in the poetic books. The most common are *similes* or explicit comparisons, in which something is said to be 'like' or 'as' something else.

Examples. 'As a father pities his children, so the Lord pities those who fear him' (Ps. 103:13). 'As a door turns

on its hinges, so does a sluggard on his bed' (Pr. 26:14).
'Like a lamb that is led to the slaughter, and like a sheep
that before its shearers is dumb, so he opened not his
mouth' (Is. 53:7). 'So I will be to them like a lion, like a
leopard I will lurk beside the way. I will fall upon them
like a bear robbed of her cubs' (Ho. 13:7 f.). 'How
often I would have gathered your children together as a
hen gathers her brood under her wings!' (Mt. 23:37).

In a *metaphor*, words of description are in a similar
way transferred to objects to which they are not literally
applicable, but the words of explicit comparison ('as',
'like') do not appear; the comparison is implicit.

Examples. 'The windows of the heavens were opened'
(Gn. 7:11). 'The Lord is my shepherd, I shall not want;
he makes me lie down in green pastures. He leads me
beside still waters' (Ps. 23:1, 2). 'Purge me with hyssop,
and I shall be clean; wash me, and I shall be whiter than
snow' (Ps. 51:7). 'So then you are no longer strangers
and sojourners, but you are fellow citizens with the
saints and members of the household of God, built upon
the foundation of the apostles and prophets, Christ
Jesus himself being the cornerstone' (Eph. 2:19, 20).

(*ii.*) *Personification and anthropomorphic language.*
This is just another form of metaphorical writing.
Personification is attributing a personality to an abstract
idea, or to something that is not personal (night, wisdom,
virtue, *etc.*); this is commonly used for dramatic effect
in poetic writing. An example is the personification of
wisdom in Proverbs 8; wisdom is spoken of as calling
out her advice by the town gates.

Anthropomorphism (from the Greek *anthrōpos*, man,
and *morphē*, shape, form) means attributing a human
form to something non-human. In the Bible, God is
often referred to anthropomorphically; he is described
at various times as having hands (Ps. 119:73), feet (Ex.

34

24:10), eyes (2 Ch. 16:9), ears (Ps. 34:15), and so on. Without such language we would not be able to understand his nature.

This use of anthropomorphic language for God is not simply a poetic device, however; the whole of the Bible speaks of a personal God who cares for man, who, in fact, made man in his own image, and who chose to reveal himself to men within their world by himself becoming man.[2] Anthropomorphic language, then, is not 'crude, semi-idolatrous thinking. It is just the opposite. It is an expression, the only effective expression, of an intense sense of the real presence and dynamic activity of the living God. It was precisely because they knew God not as a static idol or as a metaphysical theory, but as one to be reckoned with, that they used this forceful imagery.'[3]

(iii.) Parables and allegory.[4] The word 'parable' in English, as in Hebrew and New Testament Greek, can be used to refer to all sorts of figurative or proverbial sayings. Some parables are very simple sayings, others much more complicated. Some parables are little more than expanded similes; see, for example, Matthew 13:33, 'The kingdom of heaven is like leaven.' The kingdom in this sort of parable is compared to some familiar phenomenon or realistic story.

Other parables are more complicated and have several points of comparison. The parable of the sower in Matthew 13:3–9, for example, compares the four types of hearer to four types of soil (cf. Nathan's story to David in 2 Sa. 12:1–6; the parable of the vineyard in

[2] This illustrates the point, which is discussed in detail in chapter 6, that we must relate our interpretation of individual passages to the *whole* of Scripture.

[3] R. T. France, *The Living God* (IVP, 1970), p. 18.

[4] On the allegorical interpretation of the Old Testament, see below, chapter 5, section 5c.

Mt. 21:33-43; the parable of the wheat and weeds, or tares, in Mt. 13:24-30, in which almost every point has some point of comparison in the interpretation given in Mt. 13:36-43). The more complicated the correspondence between a parable and its interpretation becomes, the more 'allegorical' it is liable to be. That is to say, it is no longer a simple simile explaining one reality by comparing it with another; it is rather a story specially constructed to fit in with and to illustrate the truth that the author wishes to put over. For an example of a full-blown allegory, see the story of Oholah and Oholibah in Ezekiel 23.

The fact that there are these different types of parable makes the problem of interpretation difficult. How are we to know if we are reading a simple parable or an allegorical parable? How do we know whether or not particular elements in a parable may be interpreted allegorically? As always, we should seek to be guided by Scripture's own interpretation of Scripture. As far as parables go, we are often given some idea of how a particular parable should be interpreted. Some have argued that all Jesus' parables were intended to make a single point and no more; but this view is contradicted by the Gospels themselves (see, *e.g.*, the interpretations given in Mt. 13:18-23; 36-43), and there is no good reason to deny that Jesus may on occasion have used allegory.

Although Jesus did use parables with more than one point from time to time, however, there is no evidence to suggest that *most* of his parables were allegorical. For if the evangelists supposed that the majority of the parables were detailed allegories, we might have expected them to give their readers detailed interpretations more often than they do. Judging from the amount of interpretation that we are given in the Gospels, we may safely conclude that most parables are making relatively simple points. In seeking to interpret them, therefore, we should look for the main point in the parable and not allow ourselves to be distracted into speculations about points of detail, unless, of course, the evangelists indicate that there *is* significance in particular details.

4. Respect the rules of grammar : notice the different ways in which words are used, the form in which sentences are constructed, the way in which ideas are expressed. Attention to detail is vital.

a. Notice the 'mood' of the verbs, i.e. whether they are indicative, imperative, *etc.*

Examples. AV mistranslated John 5:39 by putting the verb in the imperative: 'search the Scriptures' instead of 'you search'.

Luke 2:29, 'Lord, now lettest thou' (AV, RSV) is often understood as though it were imperative, whereas in fact the verb is indicative: 'Lord, now you let . . . '. See NEB.

b. Notice the tenses of the verbs : are they present, imperfect (past continuous), *etc.*? In Greek the use of a certain tense may have a particular significance.

Example. 1 Corinthians 3:3 could be translated: 'I planted (aorist tense – one act), Apollos watered (aorist), but God was all the time giving the growth (imperfect – continuous action)'.

c. Notice the positions of words to give emphasis. Again, this is particularly significant in Greek.

Examples. Matthew 5:18: '*I* (emphatic) say to you.' Matthew 28:5: ' "*You*," he said, "have nothing to fear" '

37

(*i.e.* as compared with the soldiers on guard: the NEB translation of verses 4 and 5 brings this out).

d. Notice punctuation.

Examples. In John 12:27 there should be a question mark after 'Father, save me from this hour.' Compare AV and RSV.

e. Try to appreciate the underlying Hebrew and Greek idiom.[5] Note that both Hebrew and Greek ways of speaking are at times different from ours, and that Greek idiom needs to be understood by comparison with the spoken Greek current in the first century, rather than with classical Greek. This is a field of study that is continually yielding fresh insights.

Examples. The statement 'I have loved Jacob but I have hated Esau' (Mal. 1:2, 3) is the Hebrew way of stating not so much a direct opposite as a comparison; in other words, 'I loved Jacob more than Esau.' In Hebrew there are no greys; everything is either black or white.

It now appears that when Luke 15:13 says that 'the younger son gathered all he had' (RSV) it means 'he realized his estate and turned it into ready money'. NEB therefore translates it 'turned the whole of his share into cash'.

5. Get at the meaning of single words, but always study them in their setting. It is, of course, essential to under-

[5] If you do not know Hebrew or Greek the commentaries will help you. If you know Greek or Hebrew you will find useful C. F. D. Moule's *Idiom Book of New Testament Greek*[2] (CUP, 1959), as well as dictionaries, *e.g.* F. Brown, S. R. Driver, C. A. Briggs, *Hebrew and English Lexicon of the Old Testament* (OUP, 1906); W. Bauer (translated by W. F. Arndt and F. W. Gingrich), *A Greek-English Lexicon of the New Testament* (University of Chicago Press, 1957).

stand the meaning of individual words in order to grasp the full sense of a passage. Detailed word study, although it has exacting demands and inexhaustible possibilities, often throws deeper light on the meaning of a passage or of a biblical concept.

The importance of relating what you are studying to its context has already been emphasized, and this applies as much to words as to longer passages. We must let a word's setting determine its particular sense or significance, for the context of a word or statement clearly limits its meaning and prevents it from being taken in more than one sense. This is particularly relevant to words which have more than one meaning, or to phrases or statements which can be ambiguous, or even suggest an opposite idea if taken out of context.

Examples. In Joshua 24:15 the words 'Choose this day whom you will serve' refer not, as often suggested, to the choice between serving God or serving other gods, but to the choice between different false gods which must be made by those who will not serve the Lord. The rest of the verse makes this clear.

Note the different meanings of the Greek word *pistis* (faith, faithfulness, the faith) in the following four contexts. 'He . . . is now preaching the faith he once tried to destroy' (Gal. 1:23); 'Does their faithlessness nullify the faithfulness (*pistis*) of God?' (Rom. 3:3); 'For we walk by faith, not by sight' (2 Cor. 5:7); God 'had opened a door of faith to the Gentiles' (Acts 14:27).

a. Remember that words acquire a special meaning from their use in the Bible. The Bible may give a word a special sense which it does not have in the contemporary Hebrew or Greek. In any study of the prophets we shall find that, because no adequate descriptive terms for what they wanted to say existed in the language, they often had to take existing words and fill them by their use with new meanings.

Examples. The phrase 'the Lord's anointed' (in Greek *Christos*), referring originally to the anointed king, came to be a technical term for the Messiah, the king who was to come. See the progress of the word in 1 Samuel 24:10; Psalm 2:2; Acts 4:26; Revelation 11:15.

Words such as love (*agapē*), humility (*tapeinophrosynē*) and godliness (*eusebeia*) take on in the New Testament special meaning related to the Christian life that they did not have in contemporary Greek.

b. Take words in the sense in which they were intended by the original writers and as they would have been understood by the original readers or hearers. We must not try to twist words so that we make them say what we want them to say, nor must we read a modern significance into biblical words. This applies particularly, of course, to words which have modified or changed their meanings in later times. The same rule applies to the use of old translations such as the AV.

Examples. The word 'saint' has been given a different sense in the modern world from that of the New Testament, where it refers to all Christians; see, *e.g.*, Acts 9:32; Rom. 15:25; Philippians 4:22.

In the AV, 'prevent' means to 'anticipate' or 'precede' in Psalm 119: 147; 1 Thessalonians 4:15; *cf.* RSV. 'Let' means 'hinder' or 'restrain' in Isaiah 43:13; 2 Thessalonians 2:7.

c. Beware of inventing a meaning for a word, or of finding a theological significance in it, from its derivation alone. If you are careful to study words in their contexts you should not fall into this trap, but it is worth emphasizing as it is a common mistake. Although the study of the derivation of a word may throw light on its meaning and will supply details about its history, it is not a reliable guide to its present meaning, which depends on its actual use.

Example. The Greek word *ekklēsia* (church) is derived from the words *ek* (out) and *kaleō* (I call). Some people have made much of the supposed significance of *ekklēsia* as 'the called-out people'. The original writer, however, would not have had the derivation in his mind, since *ekklēsia* was the word in common use for 'assembly', and he would automatically have used it. An English example will underline the point. Although the word 'nice' derives from the Latin word *nescius* (ignorant), few people are aware of this and, if they were, it would not alter the fact that 'nice' is *used* in a totally different sense.[6]

[6] For a more detailed discussion of this example, and of the question as a whole with other examples, see James Barr, *The Semantics of Biblical Language* (OUP, 1961), especially chapter 6.

Understanding a passage
in relation to the whole Bible
5

The Christian's use of the Bible does not end when he
has succeeded in understanding a particular text. This
is in fact where the more direct Christian use begins.
For the Bible is not just a collection of ancient texts
which are studied out of antiquarian interest; it is the
Word of God to us and is meant to be a spiritual guide-
book to show us the right way, to instruct us for salvation, to enable us to know the truth by which we can be
set free and sanctified (see Rom. 15:4; 1 Cor. 10:11;
2 Tim. 3:15–17; Jn. 8:31; 17:17). If it is to serve this
practical end, the Bible must be interpreted within and
in terms of the Christian revelation as a whole. We need
to be able not only to give the original sense, but also to
discern the larger and abiding significance.

1. Recognize the divine inspiration of Scripture. The
Bible was written by human writers in human situations; but in the Christian view there is more to it than
that. Peter puts it this way, when speaking of the Old
Testament prophets: 'Men they were, but, impelled by
the Holy Spirit, they spoke the words of God' (2 Pet.
1:21, NEB). And Paul in 2 Timothy 3:16 describes
Scripture as 'inspired' or 'God-breathed'. Just as Jesus

was both man and God, so in a different but rather similar way Scripture is both human and divine. This Christian view of the Bible goes back to Jesus himself: 'to Christ the Old Testament was true, authoritative, inspired. . . . To him what Scripture said, God said.'[1] This should be the decisive argument in its favour for a follower of Christ.

The fact of divine inspiration means that Scripture is something much greater than a collection of thoughts of certain historical individuals. Although they were written at a particular time for a particular situation, the biblical writings have eternal relevance and a higher purpose than that of which the human writers will usually have been conscious. One result of this is that when we view a particular passage in the context of the whole biblical revelation, we may be able to see in it more than even the original author could have appreciated.

Examples. Some of the Old Testament prophets were aware that the divine Spirit of prophecy in them was bearing witness to things still to come, the full significance or ultimate fulfilment of which they could not grasp; see 1 Peter 1:10–12. But our position is different. We live in the light of New Testament fulfilment and so we may rightly expect to appreciate and to use parts of the Old Testament in a way which people could not do before Christ came. (An interesting passage in this connection is John 11:47–53, where the evangelist sees in the words of the high priest a far deeper significance that Caiaphas ever imagined.)

When Paul wrote his Letters to particular churches and individuals, he could scarcely have been aware that

[1] J. W. Wenham, *Christ and the Bible* (IVP, 1972), p. 12. See this book for a discussion of the authority and inspiration of Scripture.

they were intended in the divine providence to be authoritative scriptures for the whole Christian church through the ages!

We will now go on to spell out some of the ways in which our belief in inspiration will affect our handling of the Bible.

2. Recognize the unity of the biblical revelation, and aim to keep in harmony with its general tenor. The various books of the Bible are coherent parts of a single system of God-given education for the whole human race. Each part has a contribution to make to full understanding, but taken by itself it is incomplete and may even be misleading. A constant practical objective of all our Bible study, therefore, should be to get beyond the contributions of particular passages to a properly developed understanding of the consistent teaching of the Bible as a whole.[2] This will mean that we take care to read the whole of the Bible and not only favourite sections or selected portions. It will mean, too, that we read the Bible consecutively as well as undertake a more analytic study of details of particular sections.

The only way to guard against false doctrine is to keep within the circle of Scripture as a whole, and not go off at a tangent from one or two passages on the circumference. Heresies commonly start from an exaggerated interpretation of one side of truth, and no error is more misleading than one which seems to be based on truth or to be grounded in the Word of God.

3. We must compare one scripture with another, and let one scripture check the interpretation of another. We should beware of interpreting one passage in such a way that it

[2] See further below, chapter 6, section 5.

conflicts with another. Some people seem to delight in finding contradictions in the Bible and then arguing that the Bible cannot be trusted because of these contradictions. We should recognize that the different emphases and viewpoints found in different parts of Scripture are intended to complement each other and not to cancel each other out. It is by holding together the teaching of different parts of the Bible that we shall have a balanced faith and appreciate the full richness of biblical truth.

4. Interpret the obscure by the clear, and the partial reference by the more complete one. Some passages in the Bible, taken by themselves, are very obscure and hard to understand, particularly when we meet them for the first time. Their language, too, may be figurative and enigmatic; they seem to need clarification. In such cases it is important to look for some clear and more detailed scriptural statements, in order to understand them truly and not to make incomplete or abstruse statements the main foundation of what, as far as the rest of the Bible is concerned, is a novel doctrine.

Examples. You are more likely to arrive at a correct doctrine of marriage by examining Ephesians 5 and 1 Timothy 4:1–4 before 1 Corinthians 7. Revelation 20:1–6 is often made the starting-point for teaching on the second coming and other teaching made to fit in with this, whereas it would be more helpful if Jesus' own teaching on the subject were studied first.[3]

5. Use the Old Testament as a preparation, background and virtual reference book for the understanding of the

[3] These examples are taken from J. A. Balchin, 'Biblical Hermeneutics', part 1 (*Theological Students Fellowship Bulletin* 31, autumn 1961), p. 12.

New Testament. Interpret the Old Testament in relation to the New and its fulfilment in Christ. Many of the ideas in the New Testament are strange to us – sacrifice, atonement, the people of God, for example. The key to the understanding of ideas such as these lies in the Old Testament. Jesus himself was brought up as a Jew and lived as a Jew: he was circumcised on the eighth day according to the law (Lk. 2:21) and attended the synagogue regularly on the sabbath (Lk. 4:16). He was immersed in the Old Testament Scriptures, and much of his teaching, as well as that of his followers, can be fully appreciated only in the light of this Jewish background.

Just as the key to the understanding of the New Testament is an understanding of the Old, it is clear that the New Testament writers believed that the true meaning and intention of many Old Testament passages and figures could be fully understood only in the light of what God had done in the incarnation, death and resurrection of his Son, and through the consequent gift of the Spirit and the birth of a church which was to include all nations. As Augustine said, 'The New is in the Old concealed; the Old is in the New revealed.' Leviticus would not be fully understood without Hebrews. Nor would Isaiah without the Gospels. Nor would all the Bible without Christ.

The New Testament, then, is to be seen as the fulfilment of the Old. But in what ways does it fulfil the Old Testament? The New Testament's answer to this question seems to be 'In many ways'.

a. Predictive prophecy. The simplest type of fulfilment, and the one we most easily understand, is straightforward fulfilment of prediction: what the Old Testa-

46

ment author looked forward to and predicted is now happening in New Testament days.

Example. The prophet Micah predicted that 'one who is to be ruler in Israel, whose origin is from old' would come from Bethlehem (Mi. 5:2; *cf.* Mt. 2:5, 6).

b. Typology. Sometimes when the New Testament author says that part of the Old Testament is being fulfilled, he seems to see in the Old Testament a meaning that was different from, and deeper than, the one which the original author probably appreciated. When Isaiah wrote 'A young woman (or "virgin") shall conceive and bear a son' (7:14) he was almost certainly thinking of the birth of a child in his own time, who would be a sign to the people of his day. Before the child became old enough to distinguish good from evil, two enemies of Judah were to be overthrown (7:16). In this connection the prophecy made no reference to miraculous virgin birth or to divine incarnation. It simply meant that a young woman – possibly a particular one ('the virgin', RV mg.), say a princess of the royal household, and possibly one not yet married but about to be – would give birth to a son, and would express her faith in God and in the certainty of his help by calling the child 'Immanuel'. This would be her way of declaring in dark and perilous times her confidence that God was on their side (contrast 1 Sa. 4:19–22); and her faith was not to be disappointed.

In Matthew 1:22, 23, however, the same words of prophecy are taken quite differently and are applied to the birth of the Saviour Jesus. 'Emmanuel' in this case is literally true: in the person of the child Jesus God is with us. And in this case the 'virgin' is of course an unmarried woman. The birth of this child was the greatest of all God-given signs of deliverance. So in this

47

event the writer of Matthew's Gospel sees the true fulfilment and ideal realization of the words of the prophet.

This perhaps rather surprising use of the Old Testament may be most helpfully understood as a 'typological' use.[4] When the New Testament writers use the Old Testament typologically, they are not claiming that the Old Testament writers actually had the New Testament situation and fulfilment in mind; rather they are saying that the pattern of God's dealings with his people in Old Testament times is being repeated in his dealings with people in New Testament times. This is not an interesting accident, but the result of God's consistent purposeful way of acting. God acted in the Old Testament to prepare for the New Testament and for the coming of Christ, so that the history and religious ritual of the Israelites are a 'type' or a 'shadow of the good things to come' (Heb. 10:1).

Examples. In Hosea 11:1 the words 'Out of Egypt I called my son' are applied to the people of Israel at the time of the exodus. Matthew, however, refers them to Jesus (see Mt. 2:15). He sees the experiences of Israel as a 'type' of Jesus' experiences. Jesus is the true Son of God and the perfect representative of God's people.

Similarly, the Jewish sacrificial ritual is seen in the New Testament as looking forward to the sacrifice of Christ (see Heb. 4:14—5:10; 7:1—10:25). The idea of an anointed king in Israel (*e.g.*, 1 Sa. 16:6) and of the holy city, Jerusalem (see, *e.g.*, 2 Ch. 6:6; Ps. 2:6), are to stand for something higher and greater than the thing originally referred to: Jesus is supremely 'the Christ', *i.e.* the Anointed One (*e.g.*, Mt. 16:16; Rev. 11:15), and

---

[4] From the Greek *typos*, literally an 'impression' such as that left by a raised surface in wet clay, and used in the New Testament in the sense of 'pattern', 'model', *etc.* See, *e.g.*, Rom. 5:14 (where Adam is said to be a 'type' or 'pattern' of Christ); Tit. 2:7; Heb. 8:5.

Jerusalem is ultimately the heavenly city, the metropolis of all the people of God (Gal. 4:26; Rev. 3:12; 21:2, 10, 11).

A further striking example is the way that Melchizedek of Genesis 14:17–24 is regarded by Hebrews (see especially 7:1–10) as 'resembling the Son of God'.

It is not always easy to distinguish typological prophecy from predictive prophecy. The only way to decide whether a passage is a typological fulfilment or fulfilment of predictive prophecy is to examine the part of the Old Testament in question and to try to assess whether or not the author's intention was to predict what the New Testament writer speaks of.

c. Allegory. As well as interpreting the Old Testament typologically, the New Testament writers also occasionally interpret it allegorically; *i.e.* they do not just see a parallel between the Old Testament revelation and Christian revelation (as with typology), but they actually claim that an Old Testament story or saying may be taken to refer to a Christian experience.

Example. Paul in Galatians 4:21–31 sees in Hagar and Sarah and their two sons Ishmael and Isaac a picture of two covenants, the old covenant of law and the better covenant of promise.

Typological and allegorical interpretation sometimes seem strange to us, but they will probably not have seemed so strange to those in New Testament times who were familiar with Jewish methods of interpretation. Such interpretation reflects the firm conviction that God is the ultimate author and inspirer of Scripture. So far as we are concerned, we are justified in interpreting the Old Testament in this way by scriptural example and precept; but we need to employ it with great restraint, for otherwise it gives unlimited scope for arbitrary fancy and opens the door for people who are not inspired in the way in which the biblical authors were to read into Scripture almost anything they wish to see there. As a general rule, it is wise to seek scriptural authority for any typological or allegorical interpretation.[5] It is unwise to imagine that, on one's own individual responsibility, one can see figures in the Bible; the mere perception of analogy will not suffice.

d. General guidelines for interpreting prophecy.

(*i*.) *Try first to appreciate each prophecy in its original setting.* Endeavour to find out what it meant at the time to its original author and to the first hearers. For the prophets were not only messengers for all time; they were also men of their own time. God gave them a message which was intended first of all for their contemporaries. The student ought, therefore, to make it his primary goal to understand that message, to learn what God said to the prophet's own situation. Such historical understanding is of the greatest importance in its own right, and it is the starting-point and necessary preliminary for all larger understanding.

(*ii*.) *Recognize the possibility of a deeper significance than that originally understood by the prophet.* The Christian believes that the prophets were inspired by God to speak not only to their own situation but also for our learning, so that the words of the prophets have a deeper significance than either they or their hearers understood originally. In the light of the Christian revelation this deeper significance is often appreciated.[6]

Example. The Old Testament hope for God's decisive

[5] See further the following section d.
[6] See also section I of this chapter.

intervention to save his people is seen to be fulfilled in Christ's coming; see Luke 1:46–55, 68–79.

(*iii.*) *Recognize the limits of interpretation.* Prophecy is a fruitful field of fruitless speculation, and people have loved to satisfy their curiosity about the future on the basis of it. Note, therefore, (1) that God has not purposed to reveal everything. For example, our Lord made plain that it was not for men, not even for his most intimate followers, to know 'the times and seasons which the Father has fixed by his own authority' (Acts 1:7; *cf.* Mk. 13:32; Dt. 29:29).

Note (2) that biblical prophecy has a practical moral purpose and not a theoretical speculative interest; it should be interpreted accordingly. Jesus taught, for example, that his followers should 'watch' for the last day (Mt. 24:42). By that he did not mean that we should have an obsession with the future, but that we should live in the present the sort of life that would be appropriate in the final kingdom when he returns.

Note (3) that the Bible itself states that prophecy cannot always be fully understood in advance: the predictions of Jesus' first coming, though real and detailed, were not fully understood until after his coming and their fulfilment.

Note (4) that history has seen numerous different interpretations of prophecy among deviant believers.

These features should make us slow to claim too much for our own interpretation. Do not claim infallibility and do not attempt too much.

(*iv.*) *In interpreting all kinds of prophecy – prediction, typology and allegory – seek to be guided by the Scriptures on the interpretation of themselves.*

Examples. The New Testament provides many examples of the interpretation of Old Testament predictive prophecy; see, *e.g.*, John 12:14, 15 (*cf.* Zc. 9:9); Acts 2:16–21 (*cf.* Joel 2:28–32).

We have our Lord's own authority for using the story of the bronze serpent in Numbers 21:6–9 to illustrate the gospel truth that there is life in looking towards Jesus, the crucified one. See John 3:14, 15.

In Romans 5:14, Adam is explicitly said to be a 'type' of Christ, and in Galatians 4:24 (in the example of Hagar and Sarah quoted above), Paul tells us that 'this is an allegory'.

Many theologians have interpreted the Song of Solomon, which is on the face of it a straightforward human love song, as a picture of the joys of communion between the people of God and their Maker and Redeemer. Modern scholars are not, however, agreed that this is a legitimate interpretation.[7] Certainly we are given no definite indication from Scripture itself that we should interpret the book allegorically. Some, however, would argue from (for example) the New Testament use of the bride analogy for Christ and the church (see Eph. 5:31–37; *cf.* Gn. 2:24) that it is legitimate to use a similar analogy for interpreting the Song of Solomon.

7. *Regard Christ, and particularly his two comings to men, as the main subject of Scripture.* The Bible describes God's revelation of himself and his plan for the salvation of the world, and at the centre of both is Jesus Christ. So Jesus is rightly viewed as the focal point of the whole of Scripture. The Old Testament points forward to him; the Gospels describe his coming and the fulfilment of the Old Testament promise of his incarnation, death and resurrection; the rest of the New Testament looks back to his coming in history, explaining it applying it, and

[7] For a brief discussion see R. K. Harrison, *Introduction to the Old Testament* (Tyndale Press, 1970), pp. 1052 f.

showing its full significance and outworking in those who responded to him. And the whole of the New Testament looks forward to the second coming, when Jesus will return in victory to judge everyone and to bring in all its final fullness and power the promised kingdom, which was manifested in a preliminary way in his earthly ministry. The New Testament shows us how the first coming of Jesus made sense of Old Testament Scriptures which believing Jews had previously been unable to understand and piece together. In the same way the second coming will make clear to us the true meaning and significance of things that we now find hard to comprehend.

So, then, the centre of God's Word written is God's living and saving Word, Jesus Christ; without him the written Word would have no *raison d'être*. Its purpose is to give us a full and adequate understanding of the truth as it is in Jesus and, just as it requires the whole church, his body, to show forth his fullness and glory in human life today, so it requires the whole panorama of God's teaching in Scripture to give an adequate picture of his glorious fullness in human words. We should make it our constant objective, then, to learn from the Bible more of Christ and his fullness.

8. Recognize the main purpose of all Scripture : to reveal the ways of God with men, particularly sinful men. Only those who recognize this can use Scripture rightly. For the Bible makes certain fundamental assumptions and is addressed to a particular need and end. It assumes that people are God's creatures, meant to find life in fellowship with him, and yet living in revolt and separation from him. Its main purpose is to speak to such rebels not of condemnation but of mercy, and to show them God's way of providing a full salvation in Christ. It is im-

53

possible to use Scripture properly as Christians unless we first accept its diagnosis of our condition as fallen creatures and as sinners, and unless we respond by showing active interest in what God has to teach through it about his graciously provided way of redemption, present restoration and heavenly destiny for all who respond to his word of salvation.

If we keep this purpose of Scripture in mind, we shall also be prevented from expecting to find in the Bible the answer to everything. 'The wisdom it offers is saving wisdom, that is, a knowledge that is able to make us wise unto salvation (2 Tim. 3:15). So it is not able to make us wise unto biology, botany, geology. . . . Calvin says, "If you want to learn geology or any other recondite art, go elsewhere." '[8]

9. *Recognize that truth is many-sided and be prepared to accept the inevitable paradoxes that are involved in understanding infinite truth.* For example, Jesus Christ is both God and man. We must keep in mind *both* these aspects of his nature, and not emphasize only one. Similarly, for a full picture of some aspects of doctrine, we may have to accept two apparently contradictory and irreconcilable extremes. We must be careful to take into consideration the whole of Scripture teaching on a certain subject and not just a selection of texts that fit in with our particular preconceptions or point of view. For example, some may be tempted to stress the biblical teaching on predestination at the expense of its teaching on man's responsibility. Others, however, may stress human freewill and underplay the biblical doctrines of sin, election and predestination.

Charles Simeon who, at the turn of the eighteenth century, had a wide influence as an evangelical minister

[8] J. A. Balchin, *Theological Students Fellowship Bulletin* 31, p. 11.

in Cambridge, felt strongly that one's theological views should be formed from the Bible alone, and that a faithful adherence to the Bible would involve at one time embracing one 'extreme' and at another time the other 'extreme': 'The truth is not in the middle, and not in one extreme, but in both extremes.'[9] He is worth quoting at length:

'The author is disposed to think that the Scripture system is of a broader and more comprehensive character than some very dogmatical theologians are inclined to allow; and that, as wheels in a complicated machine may move in opposite directions and yet subserve one common end, so may truths apparently opposite be perfectly reconcilable with each other and equally subserve the purposes of God in the accomplishment of man's salvation. The author feels it impossible to avow too distinctly that it is an invariable rule with him to endeavour to give to every portion of the Word of God its full and proper force, without considering what scheme it favours, or whose system it is likely to advance. Of this he is sure that there is not a decided Calvinist or Arminian in the world who equally approves of the whole of Scripture . . . who, if he had been in the company of St Paul when he was writing his Epistles, would not have recommended him to alter one or other of his expressions.'[1]

10. Recognize the limits of what God has revealed. It is a mistake to expect to be made wise beyond what is written. God is a God who hides himself. 'The secret things belong to the Lord' (Dt. 29:29). In answer to a

[9] H. G. C. Moule, *Charles Simeon*[3] (IVP, 1965), p. 77.
[1] *Ibid.*, p. 79.

pressing question from his disciples, our Lord simply answered, 'It is not for you to know' (Acts 1:7). With reference to the time of his coming, he said, 'Of that day or hour no one knows' (Mk. 13:32). We must therefore be humble, not seek after knowledge which is too high for us, and honestly admit both to ourselves and to others that there are many things which we do not know and cannot know in this present life, and at best know only in part (1 Cor. 13:12).

11. Recognize the limits of our own understanding. It is important, also, to recognize that the individual's insight into truth is limited by his own progress and understanding in the Christian life. The things written cannot all be revealed to the individual learner at once. We have to grow in discernment and understanding. In a school it is impossible to teach the youngest children at the level on which one would teach final-year students. Jesus said to his disciples, 'I have yet many things to say to you, but you cannot bear them now' (Jn. 16:12; *cf.* Mk. 4:33). Similarly, he said to Peter, 'What I am doing you do not know now, but afterward you will understand' (Jn. 13:7). We must therefore recognize that our own personal moral condition and the measure of our spiritual growth also put a limit on what God can reveal to us through his Word.

Remember, too, that human understanding is finite, and our own ability to grasp the fullness of revealed truth is even more limited. It is wrong to make our own individual understanding a standard for deciding the meaning or judging the value of all parts of the Bible. There may be parts of Scripture which will never come within the range of my need or of my appreciation. There may even be some passages which are beyond the understanding of the age in which we live. But this does not mean that they ought no longer to have a place in the book that was written for the edification of all ages and all races and to meet the needs of all kinds of people.

12. Respect the judgment of other Christians, particularly the consensus of the church. It is self-deceiving for anyone to imagine that he has a monopoly of the truth. In our study and exposition of Scripture it is therefore wise to treat with respect interpretations held by others, particularly when they have long been accepted by most, if not, all, of God's people. As J. Russell Howden once said, 'If, for instance, I find myself being led to a conclusion which is in conflict with some statement in the Apostles' Creed, I shall, if I am sensible, question the accuracy of my own conclusion and be inclined to think that the Creed may be correct and I mistaken.'

It follows that, if I want to increase my own understanding of the Bible, I shall do well to make good use of the aid offered by the many published commentaries and expositions, particularly if I know them to be the work of people of faith and consecrated scholarship. On one occasion someone said to the great nineteenth-century preacher Charles Spurgeon that he had no need for commentaries since the Holy Spirit interpreted the Bible directly to him. Spurgeon replied to the effect that this was hard on the Holy Spirit, making him work overtime explaining it all over again when it had been pretty clearly covered in many commentaries! God has given teachers to his church, and, although we should not accept commentators' views uncritically, we are wrong if we despise scholarship and we are liable to miss what God has to teach us

Do not be dogmatic in matters over which the equally devout disagree. Obviously there are some matters, both of textual interpretation and of moral discernment, on which it is not possible to arrive at one final judgment. There is something to be said from the Scriptures for more than one view. While, therefore, it may be good to decide one's own personal viewpoint, it would be uncharitable and unjustifiable to assert it among one's fellow-Christians in such a way as to condemn those who hold some other view which experience shows to be equally possible.

13. Finally, in all our study of the Bible, we should remember to seek the enlightenment of the Holy Spirit. This, of course, is of primary importance. It is only by the illumination of the Spirit that we can discern, and only by his sanction or witness that we can know the certainty of revealed truth. The Holy Spirit has been given to reveal things which would otherwise be beyond the thought or imagination of men, and to give us the confidence or assurance of certain faith. He is the only Teacher able fully to expound his own inspired text-book. So if we wish to use the Bible to full advantage, we ought to do so in an attitude of conscious and continually renewed dependence on the Holy Spirit.

The Bible and Christian living

It cannot be stressed too often that the Bible is a practical book, of relevance to the individual, to the church and to society at large. In this last chapter, therefore, we shall make some suggestions about the practical application of the Bible. By following them we may hope as individuals and in community to live lives more to God's glory, and to enjoy the direct benefits which Scripture has been written to make ours. See 2 Timothy 3:15–17.

1. Regard and use the Bible as a channel of personal communication with the living God. God is a rewarder of all who diligently seek him. He is the living God who still speaks by his Spirit to the seeking soul. He speaks in and through his written Word. Through what he has revealed there of his will and character and of his saving acts in the past, he will teach us in the present about himself and ourselves. Through it we may have personal fellowship with him and experience him speaking to our souls, enlightening, convicting, assuring, guiding, restraining and encouraging us. To know our God and to hear him speaking to us in this way should be our greatest longing as we read the Bible, and we should come to it humbly and expectantly seeking him.

This personal use of the Scriptures is one which the Reformers of the sixteenth century, under the guidance of the Holy Spirit, restored to the church. One cannot do better than quote T. M. Lindsay:

'All the Reformers of the sixteenth century, whether Luther, Zwingli, or Calvin, believed that in the Scriptures God spoke to them in the same way as He had done in earlier days to His prophets and apostles. They believed that if the common people had the Scriptures in a language which they could understand, they could hear God speaking to them directly, and could go to Him for comfort, warning or instruction; and their description of what they meant by the Holy Scriptures is simply another way of saying that all believers can have access to the very presence of God. The Scriptures were therefore for them a personal rather than a dogmatic revelation. They record the experience of a fellowship with God enjoyed by His saints in past ages, which may still be shared in by the faithful. In Bible history, as the Reformers conceived it, we hear two voices – the voice of God speaking love to man, and the voice of the renewed man answering in faith to God. This communion is no dead thing belonging to a bygone past; it may be shared here and now.'[1]

2. Let the Bible tell you what to believe and do, and never assume that you know it all. The Bible is the Christian's rule of faith. If we want to know what to believe and what to do as Christians, the Bible must be our decisive court of appeal. 2 Timothy 3:16 makes the point

[1] T. M. Lindsay, *A History of the Reformation*, I (T. and T. Clark, 1906), p. 453.

clearly: Scripture has been inspired 'for teaching, for reproof, for correction, and for training in righteousness' – in other words, both for correct doctrine and for correct behaviour. The Anglican Thirty-nine Articles put it this way: 'Holy Scripture containeth all things necessary for salvation: so that whatsoever is not read therein, nor may be proved thereby, is not to be required of any man, that it should be believed as an article of the Faith, or be thought requisite or necessary to salvation.' This means that we ought always to seek scriptural ground and justification for all that we believe and do as Christians.

We should, on the other hand, beware of assuming that we ever have a final and exhaustive understanding of biblical truth. Although the Bible is in some ways like other ancient books, yet as God's own account of God's own truth it differs from all others, and none of us will ever grasp all it has to teach. God can use the same abiding Word to speak to people in new ways; its truth and treasure are inexhaustible. We should, therefore, look to God to use it to give us fresh light for fresh needs. It is a lamp to our feet and a light to our path (Ps. 119:105), and as we go along new paths it will still give light to guide us.

3. Regard the Bible as a handbook of salvation for sinful people, and seek to understand what God has done for you and for others. The Scriptures have the power to instruct us for salvation (2 Tim. 3:15) and it is important for the Christian to appreciate accurately what God has done, is doing and will do for himself and for others. Aim therefore to grasp the central truths of the gospel which are of primary importance for man's eternal well-being. Seek to understand God's way of salvation: it is something accomplished victoriously in the past by Jesus on the

61

cross (Eph. 2:8; Heb. 10:10); it is something going on in the present in the fellowship of Christian believers (1 Cor. 1:18); it is something that will be completed only in the future when Christ returns (Mt. 10:22; Rom. 5:9, 10).

Seek to understand how to grow in holiness (for example, through fellowship in the church; *cf.* the metaphor of the body in 1 Cor. 12:12–31; Eph. 4:15, 16 and elsewhere). Seek to understand the Christian hope, the goal of the Christian life to which everything is leading (1 Pet. 1:3–5). These truths are not just of academic interest, but are of the greatest relevance to us in our Christian lives day by day.

4. Seek to be able to give a biblical answer as a reason for your faith. See 1 Peter 3:15. It is important to understand God's way of salvation in Christ; it is important also to be able to explain why you believe what you do believe. This will be a strength to you in your own Christian life when difficulties and doubts arise, and it will help you to share your beliefs with a non-Christian. Think through the biblical answers to questions such as: What is the evidence for Christianity? (Examine, *e.g.*, the New Testament evidence for Jesus' resurrection.) What did Jesus teach about himself? (Get familiar with his teaching in the Gospels.) Why does God allow evil? (See, *e.g.*, the book of Job.) It is helpful to be able to quote accurately from the Bible. This requires a thorough understanding of what the Bible does teach, so that you may use it faithfully and not in a superficial or dishonest way. Good books on biblical faith and doctrine will help you to think out and understand your faith; but nothing is a substitute for your own personal study of the Bible.

5. Aim to get a grasp of biblical theology as a whole and to build up a 'systematic theology'. It is not just the biblical teaching about salvation or the biblical reasons for belief that are of relevance to the Christian. The whole of Scripture is given by God, and we must seek to arrive at a full and balanced appreciation of all that the Bible teaches on different subjects. As our knowledge of the Bible increases we become able to collect and classify its teaching under a connected series of main subjects. As we study in this way we shall increasingly be able to see the truths of Scripture as a connected whole or consistent system, and not just as a string of disconnected fragments. Then when we see a new truth or fresh aspect of a truth in Scripture, we shall be able to relate it to the rest of the teaching of Scripture. We should, of course, be careful to take each text seriously and we should avoid artificially forcing a text to fit the pattern we think appropriate. As we relate different texts to the whole testimony of Scripture, we shall begin to grasp something of God's total revelation. This is true biblical theology.

6. Recognize that the God of the Bible is not just interested in people's souls but in their bodies and in society; and seek to mould your attitudes to society accordingly. The Old Testament is full of practical instructions for the everyday life of the people of Israel, and it is a very delicate business to apply its rules for their society to our very different society. It is possible to learn from Old and New Testaments, however, certain fundamental principles that are as relevant to our world as to the world of biblical times (*e.g.*, concern for the poor and oppressed, Dt. 15:7–11; Lv. 19:9 f.; for justice, Dt. 19:15 ff.; Ezk. 45:9; Is. 59:4, 8, 9, 14, 15, *etc.*; for morality, Dt. 22:22 ff.). We should seek to base our thinking about society and our living in society on these biblical foundations.

7. Learn what the Bible teaches about the people of God and the Christian church, and live in the church accordingly. The New Testament Letters were letters to real-life churches, and the problems of these churches were not so different from the problems of churches today. Disunity (Phil. 4:2 f.; 1 Cor. 1:10 ff.), immorality (1 Cor. 5:1 ff.), false doctrine (Gal. 1:6 ff.) are still problems, and we need in our churches to heed the biblical teaching. The New Testament reminds us as individuals of our need for the church and of its need for us; it should prepare us for the fact that is often far from ideal, and it should encourage us to work for greater love and holiness and faithfulness to God among 'the brethren'.

8. Look for the spiritual truths that apply practically to your own life. If it is God who is speaking to us through the Bible, we cannot read it as detached spectators or as students who have only an academic interest in what it contains. Regard it rather as a mirror in which you can, by God's help, see both the person you are and the person you are meant to become as a child of God. Look in it first for the things that directly bear on your own needs and problems, failures and temptations, responsibilities and duties. Be prepared seriously to ask, and to face the answer to, such questions as: What may I learn here about my daily life, and how may I live it to please God?

9. Be a 'doer' of the word, and not a 'hearer' only. Having looked at yourself in God's mirror, take action! (See Jas. 1:22–25.) Seek, by God's help, to correct those things that are wrong in your life and to show your love for God by keeping his commandments. Be like the man who built his house on the rock; and beware of being deceived into the false and foolish satisfaction of knowing without doing. See Matthew 7:24–27. Be on the look-out continually for fresh things to do which the teaching of Scripture demands, but which you personally have never done before, or need to be stirred to do afresh.

10. Aim to work out a practical moral code directly related to life and circumstances. This does not mean a whole lot of meticulous rules. Jesus stressed the main principles of God's law and he attacked those legalists who lost sight of the main principles by concentrating on minute secondary points, and who made human interpretations of God's law of equal importance with that law. We must seek to emphasize, then, the main biblical principles and to keep them central. On the other hand, we must not stick to generalities and fail to apply Scripture practically. We should seek to decide, in the light of the Bible and from its teaching, the kind of action which is either right or wrong, so that we may know how we ought to act to please God and to avoid sin.

11. Give due weight to the opinions of others and to the teaching of the church; but recognize the place of individual conscience and judgment. On some practical ethical questions there are different opinions among Christians over the interpretation of Scripture. It is a mistake for any Christian to ignore the opinions of others: we are all members of each other in one body, and God has given his Spirit to all members of his church. He has also given particular gifts of teaching to particular members of the church. The individual Christian should therefore be very slow to go his own way and to ignore the views of others in the church (though churches are not and never have been infallible!). On the other hand, where Scripture does not spell out the detailed application of a principle, Christians and churches should be slow to impose their own particular application on others. Just as circumstance, social conditions and individual characteristics and qualifications continually differ, so detailed application of scriptural truth will continually vary. It will also vary from person to person: what is right for one may be wrong for another (see 1 Cor. 8:4, 7). Each person must be fully persuaded in his own mind; he should make sure his conscience is clear. Whatever does not come from faith is sin. See Acts 24:16; Romans 14:5, 14, 22, 23. And everyone should scrupulously respect the other person's conscience. There is a place for differences of opinion, whether over meat offered to idols (1 Cor. 8:1-13), over the drinking of alcohol or the question of pacifism. In this sinful world matters are rarely completely black or white, and in standing up for what they believe to be right two people of different opinions may both be standing up for some aspect of God's will and so both be glorifying God by their actions (*cf.* Rom. 14).

12. Recognize the need for continual return to, and fresh reformation according to, the Word of God. This pursuit first of the discovery and then of the doing of God's will as revealed through his Word never ends. In this life we never reach the place of final perfection. Each fresh day brings its fresh challenge. The road is uphill all the way. It is all too easy to 'lose one's first love' (*cf.* Rev. 2:4) and to slip back from the observance of standards once accepted. No one reformation can put an individual or a church permanently right; the history of Israel offers ample illustrations of this. There is constant need for a continual return to God to examine oneself afresh in the light of his Word, to be convicted of the beginnings of sinful decline, to be made aware of fresh ways in which advance in holiness and love is now possible. Only so can we press on to know the Lord, and hope to share in coming 'to mature manhood'. We must be willing again and again to submit ourselves to the searching light and compelling imperatives of the Word of God. 'The sacrifice acceptable to God is a broken spirit; a broken and a contrite heart, O God, thou wilt not despise' (Ps. 51:17).

13. Recognize that everyone is responsible to judge himself in this respect. This practical and moral application of Scripture to one's life and conduct is something which each believer is called and qualified in Christ to do for himself. This is our Christian calling, to grow up from infancy to full adult responsibility as members of God's family, to arrive at a responsible mind of our own as Christian men and women. So our first responsibility is not to compel others to conform to our reading of the Bible, nor to criticize them for failing to do so, but rather to submit ourselves to the criticism and constraint of this very standard. 'If we judged ourselves truly, we should not be judged' (1 Cor. 11:31). 'Whoever knows what is right to do and fails to do it, for him it is sin' (Jas. 4:17). 'Not every one who says to me, "Lord, Lord," shall enter the kingdom of heaven, but he who does the will of my Father who is in heaven' (Mt. 7:21).

14. Never stop seeking to make further progress in understanding and obedience. No one individual in this earthly pilgrimage ever reaches the place where he understands all, or has done everything that God requires of his children – not even Paul (*cf.* Phil. 3:12 ff.)! Rather, he is like an explorer confronted by limitless territory of which there always remains much more still to be possessed. None of us, therefore, should relax our quest as though we had arrived at full knowledge or perfect performance. There is always room and need to discover more, and then to walk in the fresh light to God's greater glory. We ought not to reckon ourselves to have arrived; we should always be reaching forward like people in hot pursuit of fuller understanding. In this way we shall, by God's grace, be among those who 'press on to know the Lord'.

Abbreviations

AV	Authorized (King James) Version of the Bible
Ch.	Chronicles
Col.	Colossians
Cor.	Corinthians
Dt.	Deuteronomy
Eph.	Ephesians
Ex.	Exodus
Ezr.	Ezra
Gal.	Galatians
Gn.	Genesis
Heb.	Hebrews
Ho.	Hosea
Is.	Isaiah
Jas.	James
Jn.	John
Lk.	Luke
Lv.	Leviticus
Mal.	Malachi
mg.	margin; some versions of the Bible give alternative readings or translations in the margin
Mi.	Micah

Mk.	Mark
Mt.	Matthew
NEB	New English Bible
Pet.	Peter
Phil.	Philippians
Pr.	Proverbs
Ps.	Psalm
Pss.	Psalms
Rev.	Revelation
Rom.	Romans
RSV	Revised Standard Version of the Bible
Ru.	Ruth
RV	Revised Version of the Bible
Sa.	Samuel
Thes.	Thessalonians
Tim.	Timothy
Tit.	Titus
Zc.	Zecharaiah

Index of Biblical references

General index

General references to biblical books are included here. For specific references, see the index of biblical references.

Revised Standard Version (RSV), 13, 37, 38, 40
Revised Version (RV), 13, 47
Ritual, Old Testament, 48

Sacrifice, 46, 48
Saint, 40
Salvation, 22, 53f., 61f., 63
Scribal errors, see Errors, scribal
Simeon, C., 54f.
Simile, 33f., 35, 36
Society, Bible and, 59, 63f.
Song of Solomon, 25, 52
Songs of Degrees or Ascents, 21
Spurgeon, C., 57
Strong, J., 14n.
Symbolism, 26, 27
Systematic theology, 63

Tenney, M. C., 18n.
Text of Bible, 12ff.

Textual criticism, see Criticism, textual
Thirty-nine Articles, 61
Timothy, 9, 11
Today's English Version (TEV), 13
Translation, 12ff.
Type, typology, 25n., 47ff., 50, 51f.

Verbs, 37
Virgin, 47

Wenham, J. W., 19n., 43n.
Wisdom literature, 22, 27f., 34
Word derivations, 40f.
pictures, 32, 33
positions, 37
study, 38f.

Young, R., 14n.

Zwingli, U., 60